Nature's Wheel

Nature's Wheel

Poems by

John Lawrence Darretta

© 2019 John Lawrence Darretta. All rights reserved.
This material may not be reproduced in any form, published,
reprinted, recorded, performed, broadcast,
rewritten or redistributed without
the explicit permission of John Lawrence Darretta.
All such actions are strictly prohibited by law.

Cover design by Shay Culligan
Cover photograph: Steven Grubiak

ISBN: 978-1-950462-38-4

Kelsay Books Inc.

kelsaybooks.com

502 S 1040 E, A119
American Fork, Utah 84003

For Steve Grubiak, trusted friend, and
my college chums, Don Spoto, and Fred McCashland,
who always encouraged me

Acknowledgments

Sincere gratitude to my family, friends, and students who read my poems throughout the years and offered their comments and suggestions that always made me rethink, revise, and move on.

With grateful acknowledgment to the publications in which the following poems (some in earlier versions) first appeared:

America Magazine: "Gli indifferenti"

The Avon Literary Review: "Nature's Wheel"

First Literary Review—East: "A Fire in the Heart," "Hot Spot Hustle"

Haiku Journal: "Haiku." Issues 42, 61, 62

The Inditer: "Deirdre in Denim"

The Journal of Pastoral Counseling: "Advent," "Sinopia for a Dream," "Sleet" (as "Askesis")

Penwood Review: "Dante's Patch," "Deconstructed"

Pilgrim Journal: "Machine"

Many thanks to Karen Kelsay and the staff at Kelsay Books for their pleasant assistance throughout the editing and publication of *Nature's Wheel*.

Contents

Prologue
Nature's Wheel — 15

I. At the Bottom

A Fire in the Heart — 19
Sinopia for a Dream — 20
"Ah! Must Thou Char the Wood....?" — 21
Gli indifferenti — 22
Sleet — 23
Ennui — 24
Dante's Patch — 25

II. Up, Down and Around

Future of the Past — 31
Deirdre in Denim — 32
Fluff and Tatters — 33
Hot Spot Hustle — 34
Learning — 35
Deconstructed — 36
Manhattan Megaliths — 37
Machine — 38

III. On the Top

Peace Move — 43
Advent — 44
Getting There — 45
After the Storm — 46
Gallivant — 47
Water Lilies by Monet — 48
Memoria — 49

Epilogue
Word Turn — 55

About the Author — 57

Prologue

Nature's Wheel

When Nature's Wheel revolves my day in light and shadow
moves wind and rain among the seasons
letting budding life of spring with stem to leaf and flower
quiver to summer's bounty at the height of the sun
then fall into autumn's amber and fade toward wintry white,
I wait for the wheel to turn again.

When Nature's Wheel surrounds my life in growth and languor
shifts depth of grief to crest of joy
making the silence or the noise with its failure or success
waver what appears today into gone tomorrow
from robe of childhood's call toward pall of pending death,
I wait for the wheel to turn again.

I.

At the Bottom

A Fire in the Heart

I shook the ashes from my hair as you covered me
with sackcloth.

You would not let me speak nor did you believe
what I had written.

I could not hear my foes or see my friends
among the clamoring crowd.

You took the letters of my name and tore them apart
ripping the love from my heart.

Together we approached the pit and only then I realized
you had never known me.

Sinopia for a Dream

I am standing
on the edge
of a cliff,
a raging sea
behind me.

There is no pigmentation.
All is unpainted
white, pure wash.
Only I am colored,
Dark.

I am moving.
I am not moving.
I can hear
the desperate cries
of the albatross.

"Ah! Must Thou Char the Wood....?"

from Francis Thompson, *The Hound of Heaven*

I went to meet
the Ash-white clouds today.

They danced for me.
We talked awhile.

Then, without warning,
the Ash-black wind came
and chased them home.

I was alone!

Gli indifferenti

The lady of the cleaners
doesn't care.
She really doesn't care.
She writes your fate
in a steamed inferno
and presses with despair.

Three pins in mouth—
Cassius, Brutus, Judas,—
she greets you low
and points with tail,
like Minos,
to where the stained
and spotted go.

"Come again," she groans
in stitched and stapled tones.
"Ma non torno vivo alcun
s'i'odo il vero!"[1]

---

[1] "But no one returns from here alive, if what I hear is true!"
—Dante's *Inferno*

Sleet

Snowflakes
semaphore and meld
in a frosty pale.

Life falls, too,
at a point
where body and soul
cross and burn,

In the place
where everything
freezes
in spirals
of dark pain.

Ennui

Last night I went out
to look for tomorrow.
I searched and searched
but could not find it.

Fog crept beside me
as I returned
to the redundancy
of all my yesterdays.

"Don't worry," you said,
"It's there."
"With hope," I said,
"I'll go again."

Dante's Patch

Twigs and leaves are bent and gnarled
and crackle to my touch
while through dry tears, I barely see
cattails burst in a flurry of used years.

there is nothing green in my land

Here in the parched lands
where all is burnt and shadowed,
I trace my fingers along a crust of earth
and crush the dust to spread on my hands
and smear across my face.

one drop of rain for the green lands

I thirst for a verdant place
where days are bright, lilies bend and sway,
and grass is moist with little beads to roll in my hands
and grace upon my face.

swiftly shooting star
cyan streaks on shadowed sky
tall treetops tremble

II.

Up, Down and Around

Future of the Past

The past is more than a memory of what was
    before it became the future.

It was that spot in time when what I could become
    moved toward what I would become.

A time to choose that and then become this
    or do this and become that?

A time to go left or right and end where
    step up or down and reach what?

It was that tick in time that starts a beginning
    and ends but to begin again.

The future is not only a turn from today
    but also a point in the past.

Deirdre in Denim

A little girl
near the old railroad house
wears a coat faded
before she was born.

Sun-dried hair
hangs around her face
of soft but saddened eyes
and dark unsettled stare.

With an absent smile
she shuffles her feet
in the dusty earth
looking for a life
    that could have been.

Fluff and Tatters

Look at the stunning starlet
perched on a satin chair.
Her lips are shiny scarlet,
streaked and fluffed the hair.
Her nails all glazed with fire,
before the curtain rises.

Look as the lady haggard
stoops to a soiled ground.
Her dirty hair is ragged,
iced fingers search around.
A crumb or two, a bone will do,
before the curtain falls.

What do we see as the world turns?
Who can it be that matters?
Is it all for shine and fluff
or just the stains and tatters?

Hot Spot Hustle

Under a lavender moon,
erotic Zelus wails a dithyramb,
as writhing Satyrs rub their buttocks
toward the hidden sun.

A black Leda flits across the floor
crying for a bird,
while tight-lipped Sibyls
shut blue-green eyes and sip white wine.

Niobe is stoned and the Gorgons laugh.

Learning

Swinging a little red lunch pail,
he studies the big fallen stump.

"What do you do with this?
It's just a funny lump."

He reads around its rings,
counting all its stages.

He pokes and finds it hard,
and will last for ages.

He pushes and pulls as if to say,
"What are you doing, blocking my way?"

He touches and jumps it,
slow circles and thumps it—

then runs off at the sound of the bell.

Deconstructed

I like to watch them split houses
and see colors climb
up and down
stairless on the wall
and think of Mondrian

to catch by twisted windows
paneless in the breeze
Wyeth awake and dreaming
in the shattered eaves

or look at roomless floors
of fallen wooden frames
to find Van Gogh
frightened in a garden
behind a broken house.

Manhattan Megaliths

I saw Stonehenge in Manhattan
where megaliths made
circles on the avenues

dawn crowded crevices
while dusty fumes
danced druid dreams

the sun tipped stone tops
and those who knew
looked up to catch the light

those who had no recollections
looked down to cluttered
gutters and reflections—
    flashing red.

Machine

With poking angles—

It cannot snake across soft sand
or curve tendrils like clematis
around a tree.

There is nothing liquid about it
not free flowing or full foaming
over smooth stone.

It cannot set and rise, slow arc across the sky
to glisten and expand in galactic circles
beyond the milky way.

Can it remember a warm fire on wintry days
the thick scent of fir and the cat curled in a "*c*"
purring near the hearth?

Does it think about its crashes, worry about collapse
turn around to see its lonely image
then feel neurotic cracks?

Whirring, whirring, whirring, broken toy circuitry
clicking and clacking down, falling flat and tinny
like a metallic clown—
What will come to save it?

smiling summer falls
autumnal leaves pale and pass
weary winter springs

III.

On the Top

Peace Move

A room emptied for moving
reveals a new start.
We gather things together
and rend them apart.

First, decorations go,
adornments long admired.
Then, old effects of pleasure,
furniture retired.

Curtains and shades are stripped,
 muddling remains are sheared.
Rugs are rolled and tied,
lingering dust is cleared.

A space, vast, vacant and serene,
streams of sun so bright.
Peace is the mind cleared of everything
      —except the light.

Advent

A Sunday morning
before Christmas
and in early shadow
clouds rain down

on silent winding gusts
a bird waits in the eaves
amid the splintered shed

then falling drops
flare out in flakes
and hemlock tufts
are soon flocked white
like lambs moving still

a horse huffs from the stable
smoke trembles along the hill

sun straining to come through
fractures dewy dawning
and quietly arrives
in a shimmering rise
of red, gold, green and blue.

Getting There

Falling deeper and deeper
down a black hole
grasping for light, holding on tight
fingertips cling to an edge of the past
remembering smiles of joy, scars of woe

fragments of light like paperweight snow
sliding down mirrors reflecting myself
shatter in pieces like flickering stars
passed strands of saints and demon snarls
beings I've known or never knew

then I see hardy plants I've grown
greening in light, flower and spread
with my precious animals
sniffing and chewing their way
running, swimming, flying
toward men and women of my life,
young and old, knowing and learning,
grasping for truth, willing to love
swirling in beginnings, endings
ending and beginning again

when so suddenly it seems
bending in the deep
a waving sea of stars
bears me up and bolts me
to a light stronger than the sun.

After the Storm

All in an orange moment
when trees stop trembling
      and rumbling clouds rest
when birds are silent
      and waters still
when roses rebound
      and honeybees teem
when earth is calming
      and sky serene
the rising sun returns again
to sing a song of creation.

Gallivant

Away the world with willow wands
scatter leaves for Sybils
and if you will let vagabonds
run down from Wiltshire hills.

But never go where rainbows end
and dancers capriole
for foot-falls follow freely there
in sordid rigmarole.

Or walk the way of Willibrord
and cross the Isle of Man
fill the world with sunlit strands
and love from Sybils' hands.

Water Lilies by Monet

Afternoon in the garden,
the artist struggles to see
then listens to the colors—
ring of floating russet
tinge of pollen splayed on rock
red and rose on fern and green.
He views and hears,
scents and tastes, feels
through nature
reflects his thoughts in time.

Over the bridge,
with eyes of the heart
Monsieur Monet caresses
and carries colors,
gathers them to his easel.
Soon brushing sounds
cross white canvass
with streaks of tint, spots of hue
bringing lilies to a pond
for all the world to see.

The sight, sound,
scent of color
touch the palette of the looker
who has never seen lilies float
on waters in Giverney.
That day is gone, Monet is gone,
but through his vanished eyes
lilies are glowing
on the ageless pond
that afternoon in the garden.

Memoria

Like pressed petals of a dead rose
even the tone of a bell fades away
but sounds are recalled

characters play and plead in memory
until the words of a story stop
yet meaning stays

breaking night turns to day again
as passing years do cease and start
with cries of cheers or tears

leaping youth outruns crawling babe
growing venerable while slow ebbing
to be born again

like falling petals of a dying rose
even time slips space
to become eternity.

Iris flaunting furls
rainbow fields of golden rings
bloom in perfumed eyes

Epilogue

Word Turn

Words are more
than syllables of sound
or lines of black on white

They are alive
spiced with scent
stroked with light or shadow
three-dimensional
gliding or dancing

They have a history of being
in meaning and emotion
not to be flubbed by fools
or curbed by sovereign seers

Words are formed from the mouth
or drawn by fingering hand
expressions of the mind
passions of the heart.

About the Author

A former metropolitan New York college professor, John Darretta now lives in his "hermitage" on Cape Cod with cats, Koi, and Cranberries. John holds a Ph.D. in English from Fordham University and has authored books and articles on American literature and Italian cinema. As Fulbright Professor to Italy, he taught at universities in Milan and Turin, where he studied Italian film at Museo Nazionale del Cinema. A specialist on Italian films of the neorealist period, his *Vittorio De Sica,* published by G. K. Hall, was the first full-length work in English on the films of the noted director.

For John, writing poetry has been a passion since high school days. His creative work has appeared in *America Magazine, Penwood Review, Avalon Literary Review, Pilgrim Journal, Haiku Journal, First Literary Review-East,* and other venues.

www.ingramcontent.com/pod-product-compliance
Lightning Source LLC
Chambersburg PA
CBHW021027090426
42738CB00007B/932